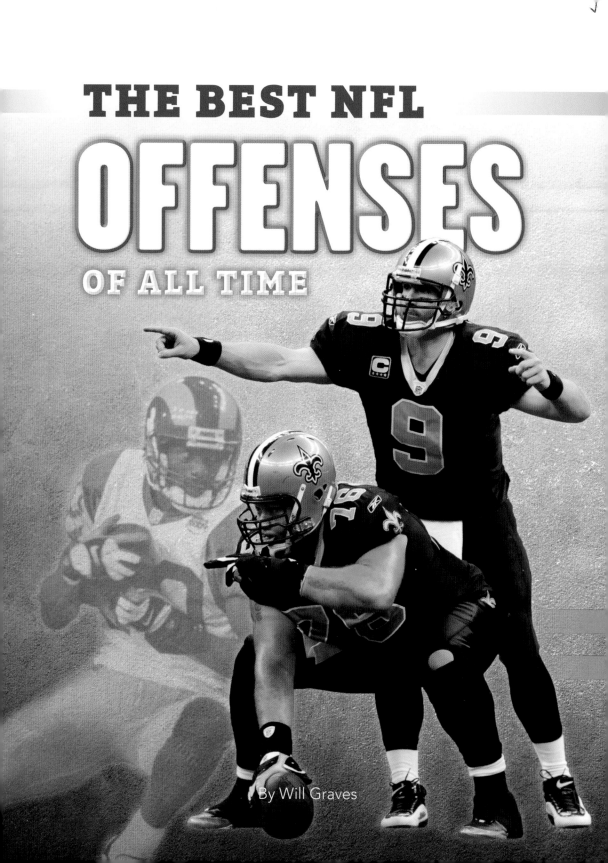

THE BEST NFL
OFFENSES
OF ALL TIME

By Will Graves

Published by ABDO Publishing Company, PO Box 398166, Minneapolis, MN 55439. Copyright © 2014 by Abdo Consulting Group, Inc. International copyrights reserved in all countries. No part of this book may be reproduced in any form without written permission from the publisher. SportsZone™ is a trademark and logo of ABDO Publishing Company.

Printed in the United States of America,
North Mankato, Minnesota

042013
112013

Editor: Chrös McDougall
Series Designer: Marie Tupy

Photo Credits: NFL Photos/AP Images, cover (left), 1 (left), 7, 11, 15, 17, 25; Bill Feig/AP Images, cover (right), 1 (right), 61; AP Images, 9, 13, 19; Paul Spinelli/AP Images, 21, 23; Reed Saxon/AP Images, 27; Jonathan Daniel/Getty Images, 29; Tom DiPace/AP Images, 31; Al Golub/AP Images, 33; Tom DiPace/AP Images, 35, 45, 59; David Stluka/AP Images, 37; Scott Boehm/AP Images, 39, 51; Carlos Osorio/AP Images, 41; Kevin Terrell/AP Images, 43; Greg Trott/AP Images, 47; Wade Payne/AP Images, 49; Michael Conroy/AP Images, 53; Winslow Townson/AP Images, 55; G. Newman Lowrance/AP Images, 57

Library of Congress Control Number: 2013931961

Cataloging-in-Publication Data
Graves, Will.
 The best NFL offenses of all time / Will Graves.
 p. cm. -- (NFL's best ever)
Includes bibliographical references and index.
ISBN 978-1-61783-909-2
1. National Football League--Juvenile literature. 2. Offense (Football)--Juvenile literature. I. Title.
796.332--dc23

2013931961

TABLE OF CONTENTS

INTRODUCTION

The goal in any football game is to score the most points. Great teams, however, do it with style and change the game forever.

The National Football League (NFL) has changed a lot since its first season in 1920. The league began as a rock'em, sock'em show with run-first offenses. Today quarterbacks are throwing the ball more than ever. The greatest offenses haven't always led to Super Bowl appearances. But they have provided fans with some breathtaking moments.

Here are some of the best offenses in NFL history.

1958
BALTIMORE
COLTS

Believe it or not, football wasn't always on TV. Johnny Unitas helped change that.

The Baltimore Colts' quarterback wasn't supposed to be a superstar. He was cut by the Pittsburgh Steelers as a rookie in 1955. The team decided Jim Finks, a former safety, was a better option at quarterback. That proved to be a big mistake.

Unitas ended up with the Baltimore Colts. Three years after being cut, he was leading the Colts into history. Unitas, running backs Alan Ameche and Lenny Moore, and wide receiver Raymond Berry helped Baltimore storm to a 9–3 record. The Colts led the NFL in points, yards, first downs, and touchdowns. Still, they saved their best performance for last.

Baltimore Colts running back Alan Ameche is carried off the field after the 1958 NFL Championship Game.

There was not yet a Super Bowl. So the Colts faced the New York Giants in the NFL Championship Game. Baltimore trailed 17–14 in the final minutes of the game. Then Unitas got to work. He put together the first nationally televised two-minute drill. Unitas connected with Berry three times on a 73-yard drive. That drive set up the tying field goal at the end of the fourth quarter.

A national TV audience followed the action from home. The game became the first in NFL history that didn't end in regulation. And Unitas made the overtime a memorable one. He drove the Colts deep into New York territory. Ameche then dove into the end zone from the 1-yard line. The game became known as "The Greatest Game Ever Played." It ushered in a new era of football on TV.

7

The number of interceptions Unitas threw in 1958, the fewest in the NFL that season.

Colts running back Alan Ameche scores the winning touchdown in the 1958 NFL Championship Game.

1958 BALTIMORE COLTS
KEY STATS AND PLAYERS

Record: 9–3

Postseason: Won the NFL Championship Game 23–17 over the New York Giants

Johnny Unitas
Position: Quarterback
Age: 25
College: University of Louisville

Alan Ameche
Position: Running Back
Age: 25
College: University of Wisconsin

Raymond Berry
Position: Wide Receiver
Age: 25
College: Southern Methodist University

Lenny Moore
Position: Running Back
Age: 25
College: Penn State University

1979
PITTSBURGH
STEELERS

The Pittsburgh Steelers rose to power in the 1970s behind their "Steel Curtain" defense. But those defensive players were getting old by the end of the decade. No big deal. Quarterback Terry Bradshaw and his buddies on offense were more than ready to help out.

Bradshaw, running back Franco Harris, and wide receivers Lynn Swann and John Stallworth kept the Steelers at the top. The offense was at its best in 1979, when it led the NFL in scoring.

The Steelers have been around since 1933. Through 2012, that 1979 season was the only time their offense led the league in scoring.

The Pittsburgh Steelers' Franco Harris runs upfield during a 1979 game against the San Diego Chargers.

Bradshaw passed for 26 touchdowns. Harris rushed for 1,186 yards and 11 touchdowns. And Swann and Stallworth proved to be too much for opposing defenses to handle. The Steelers cruised to their fourth Super Bowl appearance in six years. However, they ran into trouble against the upset-minded Los Angeles Rams in Super Bowl XIV.

Pittsburgh trailed by two points entering the fourth quarter. The Steelers needed a big play. They didn't get one; they got two. And for a change, both of them came from the offense.

Bradshaw hit Stallworth for a 73-yard touchdown pass. That gave Pittsburgh the lead. Then Bradshaw and Stallworth again hooked up for 45 yards on the Steelers' next possession. That led to a 1-yard score by Harris. The rally put the finishing touches on Pittsburgh's dynasty. And before long, Bradshaw, Stallworth, Swann, and Harris all reached the Hall of Fame.

5

The number of fourth quarter comebacks Bradshaw led in 1979, a career high and the most in the NFL that season.

Quarterback Terry Bradshaw starred while running the Steelers' offense in 1979.

1979 PITTSBURGH STEELERS
KEY STATS AND PLAYERS

Record: 12–4

Postseason: Won Super Bowl XIV 31–19 over the Los Angeles Rams

Terry Bradshaw
Position: Quarterback
Age: 31
College: Louisiana Tech University

John Stallworth
Position: Wide Receiver
Age: 27
College: Alabama A&M University

Franco Harris
Position: Running Back
Age: 29
College: Penn State University

Lynn Swann
Position: Wide Receiver
Age: 27
College: University of Southern California

1981 SAN DIEGO CHARGERS

The San Diego Chargers had just finished one of the most epic games in history. Chargers tight end Kellen Winslow was so tired he couldn't even make it back to the locker room. Playing for coach Don Coryell could do that.

The Chargers had just beaten the Miami Dolphins 41–38 in overtime in the 1981 playoffs. Winslow needed to be carried off the field by teammates. The picture of a worn-out Winslow came to be a symbol of a game—and an offense—that changed the NFL forever.

San Diego's "Air Coryell" offense called for passing, and lots of it. Coryell introduced the scheme to the NFL with the St. Louis Cardinals in 1973. However, it didn't really take off until he brought it to San Diego in 1978.

Quarterback Dan Fouts led the San Diego Chargers' "Air Coryell" offense in 1981.

By 1981 the Chargers were a well-oiled machine. Quarterback Dan Fouts flung footballs all over the field with his powerful arm. He had a dangerous group of running backs and receivers for targets. Among them were Winslow and wide receivers Charlie Joiner and Wes Chandler.

San Diego led the NFL in points and yards and finished the season 10–6. Fouts passed for a league-high 4,802 yards and 33 scores as San Diego stormed into the playoffs. The Chargers didn't make it to the Super Bowl. But their win over the Dolphins is considered one of the best games ever played. In it, Winslow caught 13 passes for 166 yards and a touchdown. And Fouts finished with 433 passing yards and three touchdowns as San Diego survived.

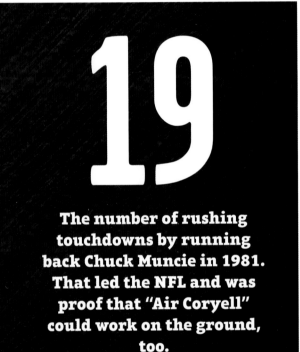

19

The number of rushing touchdowns by running back Chuck Muncie in 1981. That led the NFL and was proof that "Air Coryell" could work on the ground, too.

The Chargers' Hall of Fame tight end Kellen Winslow tries to rush past a Cincinnati Bengals defender in 1981.

1981 SAN DIEGO CHARGERS

KEY STATS AND PLAYERS

Record: 10–6

Postseason: Lost in the conference championship game 27–7 to the Cincinnati Bengals

Dan Fouts
Position: Quarterback
Age: 30
College: University of Oregon

Wes Chandler
Position: Wide Receiver
Age: 25
College: University of Florida

Charlie Joiner
Position: Wide Receiver
Age: 34
College: Grambling State University

Kellen Winslow
Position: Tight End
Age: 24
College: University of Missouri

17

1983
WASHINGTON REDSKINS

There have been faster running backs in the NFL than John Riggins. There have been stronger ones, too. Few backs, however, ran with the power that Riggins and his churning legs provided.

Riggins was called "The Diesel" because he rumbled like a Mack truck when he ran. He played behind an offensive line so big it was nicknamed "the Hogs."

The Redskins had won Super Bowl XVII the year before. The Diesel and the Hogs then set out in 1983 to show they were no fluke. And Washington recorded the league's best record at 14–2. Both of its losses came by a single point. Most of the games were mismatches.

Washington Redskins running back John Riggins was known as "The Diesel" for his powerful running style.

The Redskins scored a then-NFL-record 541 points. Riggins set a then-record with 24 rushing touchdowns. Most of them came on bruising bursts up the middle. Defenses sometimes stacked the line of scrimmage to stop Riggins. But Washington quarterback Joe Theismann made them pay. Theismann passed for a career-high 3,714 yards and 29 touchdowns. He was named the NFL's Most Valuable Player (MVP).

161

The number of points scored by kicker Mark Moseley in 1983, setting a record at the time for points in a season by a player.

Wide receiver Charlie Brown was nicknamed "Downtown" for his deep routes. He made the Pro Bowl after catching 78 passes for 1,225 yards and eight touchdowns.

Washington's bid for back-to-back championships fell short, however. The Los Angeles Raiders upset them in the Super Bowl. The Redskins came in as favorites but were crushed 38–9. The Raiders shut down Riggins and turned the Hogs into piglets with one of the biggest blowouts in Super Bowl history.

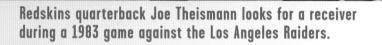

Redskins quarterback Joe Theismann looks for a receiver during a 1983 game against the Los Angeles Raiders.

1983 WASHINGTON REDSKINS

KEY STATS AND PLAYERS

Record: 14–2

Postseason: Lost in Super Bowl XVIII 38–9 to the Los Angeles Raiders

Joe Theismann

Position: Quarterback

Age: 34

College: University of Notre Dame

John Riggins

Position: Running Back

Age: 34

College: University of Kansas

Charlie Brown

Position: Wide Receiver

Age: 25

College: South Carolina State University

Joe Washington

Position: Running Back

Age: 30

College: University of Oklahoma

1984 MIAMI DOLPHINS

The Miami Dolphins selected Dan Marino in the 1983 NFL Draft. Marino and coach Don Shula seemed like an odd match at first. Miami had been a defense-first team during Shula's first 13 years there. And the formula had worked wonders. The Dolphins won two Super Bowls under Shula. But the club needed a boost after losing to the Washington Redskins in Super Bowl XVII.

The curly-haired, big-armed Marino provided one. He made the Pro Bowl as a rookie despite starting only nine games. Then he truly found his stride in 1984. The Dolphins won their first 11 games that season. They finished with a 14–2 record. Marino passed for 5,084 yards and 48 touchdowns. Wide receivers Mark Clayton and Mark Duper—nicknamed "The Marks Brothers"—both topped 1,300 receiving yards. But it was their quarterback who became the big star.

Miami Dolphins quarterback Dan Marino looks for a receiver during a 1984 game against the New York Jets.

Marino was named the NFL MVP at age 23. It marked the start of a career that would end with Marino in the Hall of Fame. Miami appeared unstoppable in the playoffs. Super Bowl XIX marked the fifth time they'd made it to the big game under Shula.

The game was one of the most-hyped in NFL history. Fans looked forward to the battle between Marino and San Francisco 49ers star quarterback Joe Montana. However, the Super Bowl proved to be a super mismatch. Marino passed for 318 yards. But he also was intercepted two times as the 49ers won 38–16. Despite Marino's amazing career statistics it ended up being his only trip to the big game.

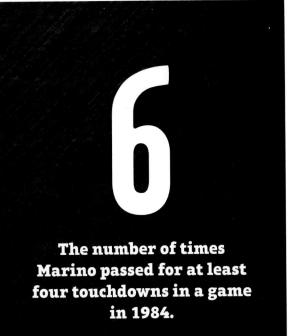

6

The number of times Marino passed for at least four touchdowns in a game in 1984.

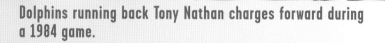

Dolphins running back Tony Nathan charges forward during a 1984 game.

1984 MIAMI DOLPHINS
KEY STATS AND PLAYERS

Record: 14–2

Postseason: Lost in Super Bowl XIX 38–16 to the San Francisco 49ers

Dan Marino
Position: Quarterback
Age: 23
College: University of Pittsburgh

Mark Clayton
Position: Wide Receiver
Age: 23
College: University of Louisville

Mark Duper
Position: Wide Receiver
Age: 25
College: Northwestern State University

Tony Nathan
Position: Running Back
Age: 28
College: University of Alabama

1988 CINCINNATI BENGALS

Ickey Woods wasn't trying to show off.
He just wanted to celebrate scoring a touchdown in style. So the Cincinnati Bengals' rookie running back took the ball in his right hand and shuffled his feet. Then he switched the ball to his left hand and did it again. He finished it off by bouncing on his right foot three times and spiking the ball. And the "Ickey Shuffle" was born.

Woods got plenty of practice while playing for the high-flying Bengals in 1988. Cincinnati scored an NFL-high 448 points. The Bengals won their division and went all the way to Super Bowl XXIII.

Woods rushed for 1,066 yards and scored 15 touchdowns. He shuffled his way to stardom.

Cincinnati Bengals quarterback Boomer Esiason hands off to running back Ickey Woods in 1988.

The NFL wasn't a fan of Ickey's celebration style, though. The league considered banning the dance from the end zone. It would force Woods to instead do it on the sideline to avoid a penalty.

The running back was just one part of a dangerous offense. The Bengals could score from anywhere. Woods and veteran running back James Brooks were a great one-two punch in the backfield. Left-handed quarterback Boomer Esiason passed for 3,572 yards and was named the NFL's MVP. And wide receiver Eddie Brown averaged an eye-popping 24.0 yards per catch.

Unfortunately for the Bengals, the "Ickey Shuffle" faded in the Super Bowl. Woods rushed for 79 yards. But he failed to score in a 20–16 loss to the San Francisco 49ers. Then he was seriously injured in 1989. Ickey was never again able to match his rookie success. He was out of football by 1992.

5.3

The number of yards per carry Woods had in 1988, the highest in the NFL.

Bengals running back James Brooks moves the ball against the Houston Oilers in a 1988 game.

1988 CINCINNATI BENGALS

Record: 12–4

Postseason: Lost in Super Bowl XXIII 20–16 to the San Francisco 49ers

Boomer Esiason

Position: Quarterback

Age: 27

College: University of Maryland

James Brooks

Position: Running Back

Age: 30

College: Auburn University

Eddie Brown

Position: Wide Receiver

Age: 26

College: University of Miami (Florida)

Ickey Woods

Position: Running Back

Age: 22

College: University of Nevada, Las Vegas

1989
SAN FRANCISCO 49ERS

The San Francisco 49ers were so good in the 1980s that it almost didn't seem fair. And that was before they got Jerry Rice.

The 49ers had already won two Super Bowls in the 1980s behind quarterback Joe Montana. They drafted Rice in 1985. San Francisco then won another Super Bowl after the 1988 season. The one thing the 49ers hadn't done was win back-to-back Super Bowls. But they did just that in 1989.

Montana and Rice dominated the league as the best quarterback-receiver duo. Montana passed for 3,521 yards and 26 touchdowns in 13 games. Rice had 82 receptions for 1,483 yards and 17 scores. The 49ers even had a future Hall of Fame quarterback on the bench. Steve Young spent most of the season as Montana's backup. However, Young did help the team win three games when Montana was sidelined by injury.

Quarterback Joe Montana led the dominant San Francisco 49ers offenses of the 1980s.

San Francisco was more than just Rice, Montana, and Young, though.

Running back Roger Craig and his always churning knees made the Pro Bowl. So did wide receiver John Taylor.

The 49ers lost just two games all season by a total of five points. They were awesome in the playoffs, winning twice to reach Super Bowl XXIV. There they had little trouble winning their fourth championship in nine years. San Francisco beat the Denver Broncos 55–10 in the Super Bowl. It was the biggest blowout in the game's history. Montana passed for five touchdowns, three of which went to Rice. The win capped off one of the greatest decades for any team in NFL history.

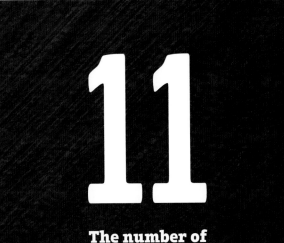

11

The number of interceptions thrown by Montana and Young combined in 1989, the fewest in the NFL.

49ers wide receiver Jerry Rice runs away from New England Patriots defenders during a 1989 game.

1989 SAN FRANCISCO 49ERS

KEY STATS AND PLAYERS

Record: 14–2

Postseason: Won Super Bowl XXIV 55–10 over the Denver Broncos

Joe Montana

Position: Quarterback

Age: 33

College: University of Notre Dame

Roger Craig

Position: Running Back

Age: 29

College: University of Nebraska

Jerry Rice

Position: Wide Receiver

Age: 27

College: Mississippi Valley State University

John Taylor

Position: Wide Receiver

Age: 27

College: Delaware State University

1996
GREEN BAY
PACKERS

Quarterback Brett Favre had a way of driving his coaches crazy. Sure, he could throw a football like the best of them. But he didn't always follow the book. Sometimes the smiling quarterback would try to squeeze a pass into a tight space. Other times he'd ignore the coaches and make his own play. This meant Favre threw some bad interceptions. But it also meant he threw some amazing touchdown passes.

Favre helped turn around the Green Bay Packers when he joined the team in 1992. In 1996, they finally became the top dog. Green Bay led the NFL in scoring. It averaged 28.5 points per game. And Favre led the way. He threw for 39 touchdowns on his way to a second straight MVP Award.

Green Bay Packers quarterback Brett Favre looks for a receiver against the San Francisco 49ers in January 1997.

The Packers weren't just a one-man show, though. Running backs Edgar Bennett and Dorsey Levens combined for more than 1,400 rushing yards. Wide receiver Antonio Freeman and tight end Keith Jackson hauled in a combined 19 touchdowns. The Packers simply lit up the scoreboard at Lambeau Field.

Favre and the Packers had some close calls in the playoffs. But they still reached Super Bowl XXXI. There they crushed the New England Patriots 35–21. It was Green Bay's first Super Bowl victory in nearly 30 years. Favre passed for 246 yards in the win. That included a 54-yard touchdown to wide receiver Andre Rison. He also had a record 81-yard touchdown pass to Freeman.

Favre started celebrating the second the ball left his hand. He took off his helmet and ran around the field, just like a child fooling around in his backyard.

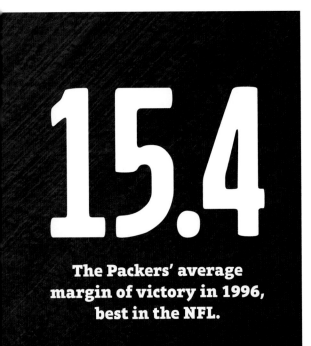

15.4

The Packers' average margin of victory in 1996, best in the NFL.

From *left*, Terry Mickens, Andre Rison, Brett Favre, and Keith Jackson celebrate a touchdown in 1996.

1996 GREEN BAY PACKERS
KEY STATS AND PLAYERS

Brett Favre
Position: Quarterback
Age: 27
College: University of Southern Mississippi

Edgar Bennett
Position: Running Back
Age: 27
College: Florida State University

Antonio Freeman
Position: Wide Receiver
Age: 24
College: Virginia Tech

Keith Jackson
Position: Tight End
Age: 31
College: University of Oklahoma

1998
MINNESOTA
VIKINGS

Randall Cunningham was at the tail end of his career in 1998. He was just hanging on as the backup quarterback for the Minnesota Vikings. That's when fate stepped in.

Starter Brad Johnson went down with an injury in the second game of the season. Critics didn't expect much when the 35-year-old Cunningham walked onto the field. Cunningham hadn't been a regular starter in three years. The days when he used his legs to dazzle defenses were long gone. Cunningham, though, still had a big-time arm. And he used it to lead the Vikings on a record-setting season.

Minnesota Vikings rookie wide receiver Randy Moss catches the ball over a defender in 1998.

Cunningham and the Vikings quickly took the NFL by storm. He threw soaring spirals to wide receivers Randy Moss and Cris Carter. Running back Robert Smith was at the top of his game. Minnesota rolled to the league's best record at 15–1. Most of the wins came in blowouts in which the Vikings ran opponents off the field.

Cunningham passed for 34 touchdowns in 15 games. Fifteen of those scores went to Moss (who had 17 total). Moss earned Rookie of the Year honors after giving defenses fits with his size and speed. Most of Moss's touchdowns came on simple plays. Cunningham would toss the ball high into the air. Moss would then jump over a defensive back and grab it like he was snatching a rebound in basketball.

The magical season did not end with a Super Bowl ring, though. The Atlanta Falcons upset the Vikings at home in the conference championship game. Atlanta won 30–27 in overtime.

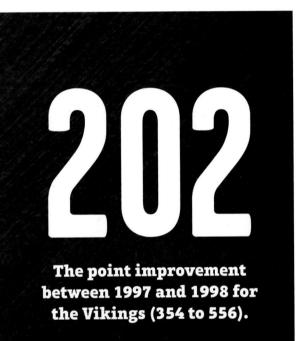

202

The point improvement between 1997 and 1998 for the Vikings (354 to 556).

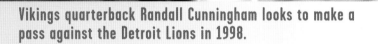

Vikings quarterback Randall Cunningham looks to make a pass against the Detroit Lions in 1998.

1998 MINNESOTA VIKINGS
KEY STATS AND PLAYERS

Record: 15–1

Postseason: Lost in the conference championship 30–27 to the Atlanta Falcons

---

Randall Cunningham

Position: Quarterback

Age: 35

College: University of Nevada, Las Vegas

Cris Carter

Position: Wide Receiver

Age: 33

College: Ohio State University

Randy Moss

Position: Wide Receiver

Age: 21

College: Marshall University

Robert Smith

Position: Running Back

Age: 26

College: Ohio State University

1998
DENVER BRONCOS

Quarterback John Elway spent the first part of his career carrying the Denver Broncos on his back. He led the team to three Super Bowls in the late 1980s. But they lost all three. Elway finally got some help when running back Terrell Davis arrived in 1995.

The Broncos finally won a Super Bowl in 1997. The 1998 Broncos proved that they weren't just a one-hit wonder. In fact, that season the Broncos had one of the most high-powered offenses of all time.

Elway and Davis forced defenses to make a tough decision. Teams could try to stop Elway and wide receivers Rod Smith and Ed McCaffrey. But that opened up room for Davis.

Denver Broncos quarterback John Elway sets up to pass against the Dallas Cowboys in 1998.

Davis, a sixth-round draft pick, had one of the finest seasons ever in 1998. He became just the fourth running back in NFL history to have more than 2,000 rushing yards in one season. That helped him become the league's MVP.

When Davis wasn't running through teams, Elway was throwing over them. The 38-year-old only played in 12 games during the regular season. Yet he passed for 22 touchdowns. The Broncos won their first 13 games before finishing the season 14–2. And the regular season was just a warm-up. Denver won its three postseason games by an average of 21 points.

Elway went out a champion in the final game of his career. The Broncos played the Atlanta Falcons in Super Bowl XXXIII. Elway passed for 336 yards and a touchdown in an easy 34–19 win. He also earned the game's MVP Award.

99.0

Bubby Brister's quarterback rating. The Broncos' backup passed for 10 touchdowns while going 4–0 as a starter after Elway was injured early in the season.

Broncos running back Terrell Davis runs against the Atlanta Falcons in Super Bowl XXXIII.

1998 DENVER BRONCOS
KEY STATS AND PLAYERS

Record: 14–2

Postseason: Won Super Bowl XXXIII 34–19 over the Atlanta Falcons

John Elway
Position: Quarterback
Age: 38
College: Stanford University

Terrell Davis
Position: Running Back
Age: 26
College: University of Georgia

Shannon Sharpe
Position: Tight End
Age: 30
College: Savannah State University

Rod Smith
Position: Wide Receiver
Age: 28
College: Missouri Southern State University

1999
ST. LOUIS
RAMS

Kurt Warner wasn't drafted coming out of college at the University of Northern Iowa. Instead, he spent time playing arena football and stocking shelves in grocery stores while keeping his NFL dream alive. Those dreams came true in 1999. Warner and his St. Louis Rams teammates became "The Greatest Show on Turf."

Starting quarterback Trent Green hurt his knee in a preseason game. Warner was called to fill in. The Rams had been among the NFL's worst teams for a decade. But they suddenly caught fire behind their unlikely superstar.

St. Louis Rams quarterback Kurt Warner takes a snap during a 1999 game against the San Francisco 49ers.

St. Louis won its first six games. Every win was by at least 17 points.

The Rams finished the season with a 13–3 record. Defenses didn't know what to make of Warner. The quarterback used the quick release he learned while playing in the Arena Football League to stun opponents.

It helped that Warner had so many talented players around him. Running back Marshall Faulk and wide receivers Isaac Bruce and Torry Holt combined to score 30 touchdowns. Warner passed for 41 scores. That was the most in the NFL. Warner was named the league's MVP.

The Rams won two playoff games to reach Super Bowl XXXIV. There, Warner and company capped their magical season with one more big-time play. The score was tied at 16 in the fourth quarter. Warner hit Bruce for a 73-yard touchdown to give St. Louis its first Super Bowl win. The Rams made it back to the Super Bowl two years later, too.

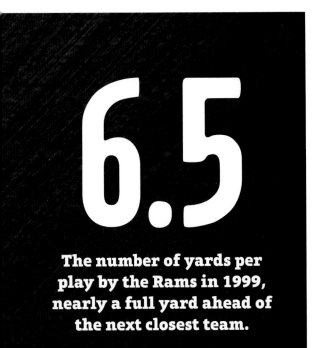

6.5

The number of yards per play by the Rams in 1999, nearly a full yard ahead of the next closest team.

Rams running back Marshall Faulk runs away from
Tennessee Titans defenders during a 1999 game.

1999 ST. LOUIS RAMS
KEY STATS AND PLAYERS

Record: 13–3

Postseason: Won Super Bowl XXXIV 23–16 over the Tennessee Titans

Kurt Warner

Position: Quarterback

Age: 28

College: University of Northern
Iowa

Marshall Faulk

Position: Running Back

Age: 26

College: San Diego State
University

Isaac Bruce

Position: Wide Receiver

Age: 27

College: University of Memphis

Torry Holt

Position: Wide Receiver

Age: 23

College: North Carolina State
University

2004 INDIANAPOLIS COLTS

Dan Marino's NFL-record 48 touchdown passes in 1984 was thought to be unbreakable. Then Peyton Manning arrived. The Indianapolis Colts' quarterback was the first pick in the 1998 NFL Draft. He already was one of the league's top players in 2004. Manning took it up a level that fall with the help of his teammates Marvin Harrison, Reggie Wayne, and Edgerrin James.

Harrison and Wayne gave Manning two of the NFL's best wide receivers as targets. Running back James was at the top of his game, too. He made defenses pay if they tried to load up the secondary to stop Manning. The result was a series of high-scoring, heart-pumping wins. The Colts averaged an NFL-best 32.6 points per game.

Indianapolis Colts quarterback Peyton Manning drops back to pass against the Oakland Raiders in 2004.

Manning's run at Marino's record heated up as the season wore on.

Manning tossed a career-high six touchdowns in a 41–9 win over the Detroit Lions on Thanksgiving. They simply kept coming.

Manning needed two touchdowns to break the record heading into Week 15. He did it in spectacular fashion. The Colts trailed the San Diego Chargers by eight late in the fourth quarter. Manning led a last-second drive toward the end zone. He hit Brandon Stokley for a 21-yard touchdown pass that helped tie the game. The score was Manning's forty-ninth of the season, a new record. The Colts went on to win in overtime.

The dream season ended when the New England Patriots beat the Colts 20–3 in the second round of the playoffs. It was the only time all season the Colts didn't score a touchdown in a game.

14

The number of games in which Manning threw multiple touchdown passes in 2004.

Colts wide receiver Marvin Harrison makes a tip-toe touchdown catch against the Tennessee Titans in 2004.

2004 INDIANAPOLIS COLTS
KEY STATS AND PLAYERS

Record: 12–4

Postseason: Lost 20–3 to the New England Patriots in the second round of the playoffs

Peyton Manning
Position: Quarterback
Age: 28
College: University of Tennessee

Marvin Harrison
Position: Wide Receiver
Age: 32
College: Syracuse University

Edgerrin James
Position: Running Back
Age: 26
College: University of Miami (Florida)

Reggie Wayne
Position: Wide Receiver
Age: 26
College: University of Miami (Florida)

2007
NEW ENGLAND PATRIOTS

Tom Brady had already led the New England Patriots to three Super Bowls.
Then in 2007 wide receiver Randy Moss arrived. The results were a match made in football heaven.

Brady's right arm and Moss's speed and size were an unstoppable combination. The Patriots went 16–0 in the regular season. Only the 1972 Miami Dolphins had previously gone undefeated in the Super Bowl era. Brady and Moss helped New England break all sorts of NFL records. Brady's 50 touchdown passes set a new single season mark. And Moss caught 23 of those touchdown passes, which was another record. As a team, the Patriots scored a record 589 points and averaged nearly 37 points per game. That was better than one touchdown more per game than the second-highest scoring team in the league.

New England Patriots quarterback Tom Brady throws the ball during a 2007 game against the Washington Redskins.

The Patriots' most memorable moment came in the regular season finale against the New York Giants.

New England trailed by five points in the fourth quarter. Brady tried to hit Moss with a bomb down the right sideline. But the pass was just overthrown. No big deal. Brady again went deep to Moss on the very next play. This time it worked, giving the Patriots the lead for good.

The two teams met in a rematch at Super Bowl XLII. But the Patriots' high-powered offense sputtered and New York pulled off a 17–14 upset. The season didn't end with a title. Still, it cemented Brady's place in football history. There was no question that he was one of the best quarterbacks of all time.

12

The number of games in which the Patriots won by at least 10 points in 2007. No team had ever won that many games by double digits in a single season.

The Patriots' Randy Moss reaches out for a one-handed catch against the Miami Dolphins in 2007.

2007 NEW ENGLAND PATRIOTS
KEY STATS AND PLAYERS

Record: 16–0

Postseason: Lost Super Bowl XLII 17–14 to New York Giants

Tom Brady	**Randy Moss**
Position: Quarterback	**Position:** Wide Receiver
Age: 30	**Age:** 30
College: University of Michigan	**College:** Marshall University
Laurence Maroney	**Wes Welker**
Position: Running Back	**Position:** Wide Receiver
Age: 22	**Age:** 26
College: University of Minnesota	**College:** Texas Tech University

2009
NEW ORLEANS SAINTS

At just 6 feet tall, Drew Brees is short for an NFL quarterback. Still, he found a way to stand tall in New Orleans.

The Saints were one of the NFL's worst teams when Brees arrived in 2006. New Orleans had won just three games in 2005. And in just four seasons, Brees turned the Saints into Super Bowl XLIV champions.

Brees led an offense that picked apart opponents on its way to the club's first title. The quarterback made up for his lack of height by being one of the smartest quarterbacks in football. He almost always made the right decision, and the Saints took off.

Saints quarterback Drew Brees gets ready to fire a pass against the Miami Dolphins in 2009.

New Orleans won its first 13 games to roll to a division title. Brees completed 71 percent of his passes for 4,388 yards and 34 touchdowns. And he wasn't picky. Brees didn't have a favorite wide receiver. Instead he spread the ball around. That meant defenses couldn't key on one person. Brees threw touchdowns to 10 different players that season. Seven New Orleans receivers caught at least 35 passes.

The Saints led the NFL in yards and points but stumbled at the end of the season. They lost their final three games and appeared to be in trouble. But that appearance soon proved to be false. The Saints crushed the Arizona Cardinals and edged the Minnesota Vikings to get to the Super Bowl. There they beat the Indianapolis Colts 31–17. Brees led the way, throwing two touchdowns in the second half as New Orleans rallied to victory.

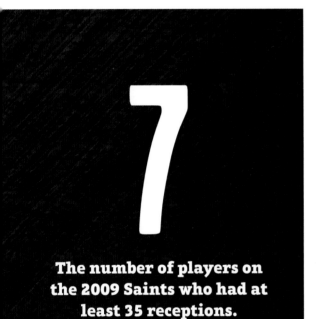

7

The number of players on the 2009 Saints who had at least 35 receptions.

Saints wide receiver Marques Colston tries to break away from a Tampa Bay Buccaneers defender during a 2009 game.

2009 NEW ORLEANS SAINTS
KEY STATS AND PLAYERS

Record: 13–3

Postseason: Won Super Bowl XLIV 31–17 over the Indianapolis Colts

Drew Brees
Position: Quarterback
Age: 30
College: Purdue University

Robert Meacham
Position: Wide Receiver
Age: 25
College: University of Tennessee

Marques Colston
Position: Wide Receiver
Age: 26
College: Hofstra University

Pierre Thomas
Position: Running Back
Age: 25
College: University of Illinois

SHAPING THE GAME

Offense in football has changed over the years. Here are some of the offensive schemes that have revolutionized the NFL.

No-Huddle Offense – In this scheme, the offense never huddles. Instead, the players stand at the line of scrimmage before each play and listen to the quarterback. The quarterback looks over the defense and then decides a play to call. Peyton Manning and Tom Brady are some of the best in the NFL at using the no-huddle.

Read-Option/Spread Offense – Used heavily in college, this scheme spread to the NFL around 2010. It works best with a quarterback who can run, because it helps keep defenses on their toes. Washington Redskins quarterback Robert Griffin III and San Francisco 49ers quarterback Colin Kaepernick used it to lead their teams to the playoffs in 2012.

Run-and-Shoot Offense – Made popular by the Houston Oilers and the Detroit Lions in the 1980s and early 1990s, this scheme calls for using four wide receivers on every play, with one running back and no tight ends. Oilers quarterback Warren Moon used it to break records and reach the Hall of Fame.

West Coast Offense – Developed in the 1980s by former San Francisco 49ers coach Bill Walsh, the West Coast Offense focuses on throwing short, accurate passes. The goal is to get the ball to wide receivers quickly. That lets the receivers get moving through the defense. The passes also are less risky than deep throws that could get intercepted.

GLOSSARY

draft
A system used by professional sports leagues to select new players in order to spread incoming talent among all teams. The NFL Draft is held each April.

dynasty
A team that wins several titles over a short period of time.

playoffs
A series of single-elimination games amongst the best teams after the regular season that determines which two teams meet in the Super Bowl.

rookie
A first-year player in the NFL.

routes
The paths in which a receiver is supposed to run in a given football play.

scheme
A system of offense or defense.

two-minute drill
A fast-paced offensive drive meant to take a team down the field for a score with less than two minutes remaining in the half or game.

veteran
A player with years of experience.

FOR MORE INFORMATION

Further Readings

Gramling, Gary. *Sports Illustrated Kids 1st and 10: Top 10 Lists of Everything in Football*. New York: Sports Illustrated, 2011.

Jacobs, Greg. *The Everything Kids Football Book, Third Edition*. New York: F+W Media, 2012.

Polzer, Tim. *NFL Reader: Perfect Passers*. New York: Scholastic Inc., 2010.

Web Links

To learn more about the NFL's best offenses, visit ABDO Publishing Company online at **www.abdopublishing.com**. Web sites about the NFL's best offenses are featured on our Book Links page. These links are routinely monitored and updated to provide the most current information available.

INDEX

ABOUT THE AUTHOR

Will Graves got hooked on football when he was eight years old, watching the Washington Redskins win their first Super Bowl. He's covered sports since 1996, and he joined the Associated Press in 2005. He currently works in Pittsburgh, Pennsylvania, where he writes about the Pittsburgh Steelers but still finds time to cheer on the Redskins every Sunday.